IN OLD PHOTOGR

TOTNES
PAST & PRESENT

DAVID F. VODDEN

SUTTON PUBLISHING

Sutton Publishing Limited
Phoenix Mill · Thrupp · Stroud
Gloucestershire · GL5 2BU

First published 2004

Title page photograph: Eastgate, 1950.

British Library Cataloguing in Publication Data
A catalogue record for this book is available from the
British Library.

ISBN 0-7509-3758-0

Typeset in 10.5/13.5 Photina.
Typesetting and origination by
Sutton Publishing Limited.
Printed and bound in England by
J.H. Haynes & Co. Ltd, Sparkford.

To the late C.D.T. Owen MA
(Headmaster)
and the staff of
King Edward VI Grammar School,
1945–52.

CONTENTS

The River Dart from the castle in 2000 shows how housing and shops with interesting gabled roofs closely at the foot of the castle motte. (*D.F. Vodden*)

FOREWORD

It is evident on reading this book that the memories portrayed of school years, of Totnes and its long history, and of its glorious countryside are, as the author has said, 'an affair of the heart' for him.

We Totnesians, I am sure, will share the views expressed and our own personal memories will be re-kindled. We are all aware of the great changes that have happened since the 1950s: the loss of Harris's Bacon Factory and of Reeves's Timberyard; the emergence of Safeway, Somerfield and of Unigate at the former Daws's Creamery; the changed status of Totnes Council; the renaming and relocation of King Edward VI School; town fires destroying the Civic Hall, St John's, Bridgetown, buildings in Warlands and on The Plains, as well as, most famously, the Eastgate. So it is timely for us to be reminded of past years and for the students of today to hear of school days at that time.

The founding of the school by Edward VI and the building of the Guildhall 450 years ago are indeed a cause for celebration and pride. David Vodden by his book has most enjoyably enhanced this pride.

William Bennett MBE
Borough Mayor 1969,
Town Mayor 1977, 1996,
Honoured Citizen

Mayor Bill Bennett revived the ceremony of Beating the Bounds in 1977. He is seen here leading procession through the Eastgate down Fore Street. (*W.C. Bennett*)

INTRODUCTION

My love affair with Totnes began when I saw it for the first time immediately after the Second World War when I became a boarder at King Edward VI Grammar School (KEVI). For seven years I grew up, enjoying not only life at school, but also the surrounding countryside, towns and villages extending over quite a wide area. Although, as boarders, we were kept close to the school, there were opportunities for exploring. For example, we were taken on longish Sunday afternoon walks by masters; there was the gruelling annual cross-country race preceded by practice runs, away sports fixtures with other schools, colleges and Forces establishments. Membership of the 1st Totnes Scout Troop also brought with it weekend camps, especially those near Salcombe.

In my second year at the school I obtained my first camera through a playground swap. It was a Baby Brownie taking 127 film. Fortunately I preserved all my negatives from then and have done so ever since. They have provided the starting point for this book in which I compare past and present as often as possible; so this book contains a collection of pictures which illustrate the recent history of Totnes, King Edward VI Grammar School and the surrounding area, mainly since the end of the Second World War.

Totnes has a very long recorded history, dating back to its establishment as a Saxon burh or fortified town on the hill above the River Dart in about 896–99. From this position the inhabitants were able to look out for invaders sailing up from the mouth of the Dart. It stands at the highest navigable point from the sea and even today there are still fine views from the castle of the River Dart downstream from Totnes Bridge.

I have chosen to approach the town from the river by looking first at the wharfs, quays, The Plains, boats on the water, Vire Island, surrounding buildings and the view of the town and its castle from the bridge. From this angle Professor W.G. Hoskins wrote of Totnes 'next to Exeter and Plymouth, the most interesting town in Devon, a lively little place . . . on a hill rising from the west bank of the Dart'.

From the Royal Seven Stars Hotel, Fore Street begins rising up, past my old school on the left which has just celebrated the 450th anniversary of King Edward VI's charter of 1553. And so to the Eastgate, at which point the name changes to High Street and we are within the Saxon burh and medieval town. Past the mainly

The Anne of Cleeves tea shop and Fore Street leading up to the Eastgate, 1975. Kerbside parking is now restricted to the right-hand side of the street. (*D.F. Vodden*)

fifteenth-century parish church and sixteenth-century Guildhall behind it and the pillared Butterwalk, the town rises up to the foot of the Norman motte and bailey castle. Understandably the High Street changes its name to 'The Narrows' at this point and squeezes past the archway entrance to the former Tucker's Toffee factory, redeveloped for housing as Castle Close. Further along is the Rotherfold, the ancient site of the cattle market.

Retracing our steps to the castle, from its ramparts there are splendid wide views of the town and river to the east, while the railway station and milk factory are to the north with Dartmoor in the background.

Also to the north, and only 2 miles away, is the very attractive Dartington Hall estate and, beyond that, but not visible from Totnes, are Buckfastleigh and Widecombe-in-the-Moor, all of which I was able to explore in the years just after the war. Although they have changed in minor ways they have lost none of their attractiveness.

I hope that my retracing the history of Totnes, largely since the Second World War, will revive many happy memories for those who have known the town since then, and prove a fascinating introduction for readers who have only recently met 'the good town of Totnes'.

David F. Vodden BA, MPhil, FRSA, LRPS

1

*The Riverside &
The Plains*

Totnes stands at the highest navigable point on the River Dart, and this view from
Steamer Quay looks across to Baltic Wharf as it is today. The old warehouse is now
converted into apartments alongside the thriving Steam Packet Inn. (*D.F. Vodden*)

I took this view from Steamer Quay looking across to Baltic Wharf in 1949. A crew from the boat club
practising on the river that evening and the Boy Scout to the left of the picture was, I think, J.R. Warn fr
Collaton St Mary, a boarder at King Edward VI School and a member of the 1st Totnes troop. (*D.F. Vodden*

This view of Baltic Wharf dates from 1981 and illustrates the timber trade carried on there by F.J. Reev
the far left. (*A.T. Lincoln*)

s view of Reeves's Timber Yard shows it at a peak of activity in September 1981. Yet within a few years
ves closed down and the wharf is now home to boat builders and to some domestic housing. (*A.T. Lincoln*)

from Vire Island are two ships unloading at Baltic Wharf. (*A.T. Lincoln*)

Longmarsh, 2003. It runs along the north bank of the river opposite Baltic Wharf and further seaward was once managed as a saltmarsh pasture but from 1860 until the end of the Second World War it was as a rifle range, firstly by the Totnes Rifle Volunteers and then by regular and Allied troops. (*D.F. Vodden*)

This is a privately owned steam paddler moored by Steamer Quay. There is a society for them and years ago several of the Society members came to Totnes. Bill Bennett and others were given what prov be very pleasant rides in the steam paddlers. (*A.T. Lincoln*)

Dartmouth Castle pleasure boat taking on passengers at Steamer Quay in 1983. Such trips began in ̇6 and continue to be very popular in the summer, although the paddle steamers are no longer in ce. The pleasure boats cruise the river down to Dartmouth via Greenway. (*A.T. Lincoln*)

 ̇r Bill Bennett MBE launching *Silver Dart* for the rowing club in 1978. The Totnes tradition was to ̇h boats using locally made cider. (*W.C. Bennett*)

In 2000 the ocean-going catamaran *Team Phillips*, built Totnes, was launched and prepared for its ill-fated maiden voyage – which came to a dramatic end when a section snapped off the port bow. Large numbers had come to Baltic Wharf to see her under construction, and a small crowd had gathered to see her enter water. (*D.F. Vodden*)

This view upriver towards the bridge shows dinghies moored beyond Reeves's timber yard and near Island. (*A.T. Lincoln*)

● Tough Mudder competitors Lisa Whitwham, Rachel Tomalin, Jodie Collins, Olivia Potter and Mark Deluce

It's muddy hell for charity fundraisers

A GROUP of fitness enthusiasts went through the pain barrier in a challenge described as the 'ultimate workout' to raise money for St Ann's Hospice.

Gym members who train at The Village Hotel in Cheadle raised more than £1,200 by taking part in a Tough Mudder event at Cholmondeley, in Cheshire.

The notoriously gruelling challenge is a 10-12 mile obstacle course designed to test physical strength and mental grit.

For many the flu can prove just unpleasant but those 'at risk' may be more susceptible to an increase in complications.

For pensioners, expectant mums or those with an underlying medical condition such as chronic heart, liver or respiratory disease, the flu virus can be life threatening so the NHS offers these people a free vaccination.

Councillor John Pantall, Stockport Council's executive member for

£20k fine f

A LAUNDRY firm has been fined £20,000 after a worker fell through the floor and onto an industrial iron suffering third-degree burns.

The 34-year-old was an employee at Vineshield Professional Services, on the Adswood Industrial Estate, when the accident happened.

Trafford Magistrates Court heard the dad-of-one fell through a mezzanine floor and was

early morning view of dinghies moored by the island at high tide in June 1989. (*A.T. Lincoln*)

s a view from the bridge of an Elizabethan craft fair, held on Vire Island in 2000. During my boyhood
s always known as simply 'The Island', but after Totnes twinned with Vire in Normandy in 1973 it
ne Vire Island. (*D.F. Vodden*)

The south side of Vire church. Totnes had failed to twin successfully with Orbec in Brittany, so Stan Caldwell, French master at King Edward VI School, suggested that the town council arrange an official twinning with their opposite numbers at Vire in Normandy. This has proved very successful and includes exchange visits between KEVICC pupils and French schoolchildren. (*D.F. Vodden*)

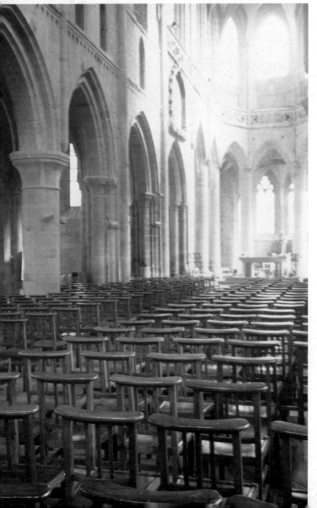

The Romanesque and Gothic interior of Vire church, which is a contrast with the late medieval St Mary's Priory Church, Totnes, with its own impressive fifteenth-century stone screen (see pages 94–5). (*D.F. Vodden*)

The ruins of Vire Chateau show that it was a later building than the better-preserved shell keep of Totnes Castle. (*D.F. Vodden*)

Like Totnes, Vire was a walled town with a castle. This is Vire gatehouse, formerly a main entrance into the town through the defences, but different in style from Eastgate, Totnes (see pages 33–4). (*D.F. Vodden*)

Totnes, seen from the bridge which was built in 1826–8. The Tollgates at the town end were removed 31 October 1881, and burnt on a bonfire at the Town Marsh. (*Totnes Image Bank*)

Totnes from the bridge shows the town still dominated by castle and church, 2003. The building on right which formed part of Harrisons' Garage has been retained as part of the newly built Bridge Te apartment block (see page 20). (*D.F. Vodden*)

...risons' Garage from the bridge with stone cottage alongside. (*Barry Weekes/Totnes Image Bank*)

...olition of Harrisons' Garage was well under way, and the site was almost ready to start the construction
...dge Terrace, March 2000. (*D.F. Vodden*)

The site of the former Harrisons' Garage with the stone cottage still standing and awaiting refurbishm
Over the other side of the bridge, St John's Bridgetown tower can just be seen. (*D.F. Vodden*)

The elegant apartment block, Bridge Terrace, 2003. (*D.F. Vodden*)

e Town Mill now houses
Tourist Information
tre as well as the
adquarters of the Totnes
age Bank. In the
eteenth century William
e owned the mill, and
re is a painting of it by
grandson Tecwyn Cole
rgan in the Elizabethan
ase Museum in Fore
eet. (*D.F. Vodden*)

way's supermarket
pies the site of the
er C. & T. Harris's
n factory, which had
established there in
0 and closed in the
0s. (*D.F. Vodden*)

The Granary Flats at Safeway's underwent refurbishment in 2003. The building had been a granary du
the Crimean War, 1854–6. (*D.F. Vodden*)

C. & T. Harris's Bacon Factory in 1969. (*E. Morrison/Totnes Image Bank*)

Mayor, W.C. Bennett MBE, with the Lord
enant, Lord Roborough, on The Plains in the
n's Silver Jubilee Year, 1977. (*W.C. Bennett*)

The Wills's memorial which could be seen in
the background of the previous picture
commemorates William John Wills and his
friend Robert Burke who were the first to
cross the Australian continent in 1861. His
birthplace, 3 The Plains, is now a restaurant
known as Wills. (*D.F. Vodden*)

IN HONOR OF
WILLIAM JOHN WILLS,
NATIVE OF TOTNES.
THE FIRST WITH BURKE TO CROSS THE
AUSTRALIAN CONTINENT
HE PERISHED IN RETURNING 28TH JUNE.
1861.
ERECTED BY PUBLIC SUBSCRIPTION
AUGUST 1864.

The Dartington Morris Men performing on The Plains in the 1980s, wearing the White Hart badg
Dartington Hall. (*A.T. Lincoln*)

The Dartington Morris Men on The Plains, 1982. They were led by Eric Langsford and accompani
Rene Tope on the accordion. (*A.T. Lincoln*)

is the riverside café in the 1980s. The site had been acquired through a legacy from former mayor and ...itect, Douglas Mitchell. Harrison Sutton Partnership produced this imaginative scheme for the Totnes ...ervation Trust. (*A.T. Lincoln*)

...stored winch at the café. Money raised from this development enabled the Totnes Preservation Trust ...ore the Town Mill. (St John's Church, Bridgetown, can be seen in the background. It has been rebuilt ...ing an arson attack in 1976.) (*A.T. Lincoln*)

Totnes has suffered a number of fires. This is a fire at Reeves's Finishing Plant in Warlands in 1
(*A.T. Lincoln*)

Warlands new houses on the site of the former Reeves's building, 2003. (*D.F. Vodden*)

Plains, before it was smartened up with attractive new housing, used to lead down to F.J. Reeves's
er sheds. Even the former chapel, which had housed Symons's Cider works on the far left of the picture,
been converted to housing. (*A.T. Lincoln*)

s a group of warehouses on The Plains, *c.* 1900. Holman's were corn merchants, also selling oil, coke,
manure, hay and straw. Because of such commercial activity a special railway branch line was laid
otnes station. (*A.T. Lincoln*)

The Dart Vale Harriers traditional meet on Boxing Day at the Seven Stars before riding up through the
via the Eastgate. (*A.T. Lincoln*)

2

Fore Street

Looking up Fore Street from The Plains by the Seven Stars. This charming print is from a collotype of *c.* 1900. (*A.T. Lincoln collection*)

Fore Street from the porch of the Seven Stars: a typical day in 1950. (*D.F. Vodden*)

Fore Street from the same place fifty years later in 2000; there are changes in the retailers and certain increase in kerbside parking! (*D.F. Vodden*)

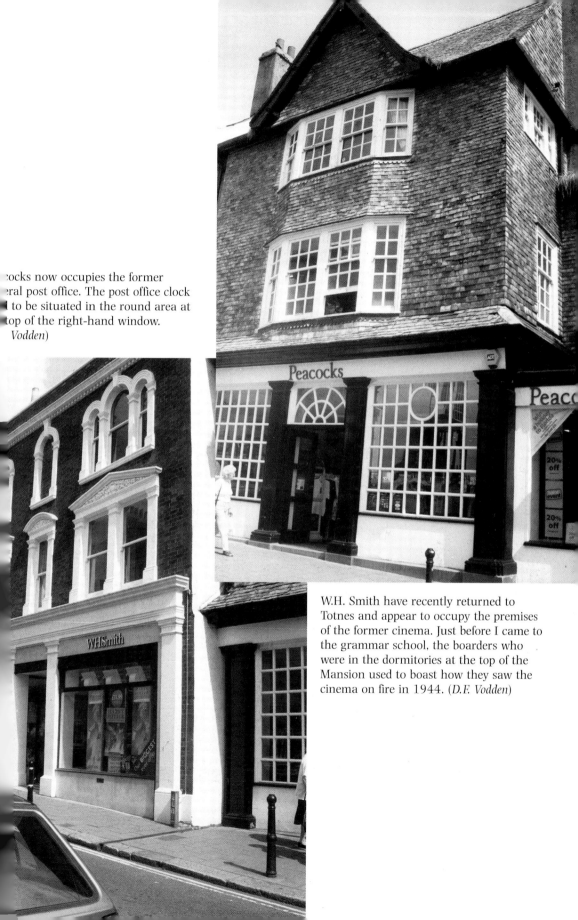

...ocks now occupies the former ...eral post office. The post office clock ...I to be situated in the round area at ...top of the right-hand window. *...Vodden*)

W.H. Smith have recently returned to Totnes and appear to occupy the premises of the former cinema. Just before I came to the grammar school, the boarders who were in the dormitories at the top of the Mansion used to boast how they saw the cinema on fire in 1944. (*D.F. Vodden*)

This 1985 view is from the public right of way which runs through the Gothic House. It is an eighteenth-century house in Strawberry Hill gothic revival style derived from Horace Walpole's prototype Strawberry Hill House at Twickenham, now a Roman Catholic College. (*D.F. Vodden*)

The Gothic House in 1985. Since then the tree in the front garden has grown and hidden the house. It is occupied by Smith and Watson Production. (*D.F. Vodden*)

The Eastgate in 1950. It has been Totnes's best-known landmark for a long time. The earliest known reference to a gate on this site is *c.* 1250. Until 1837, the beginning of Victoria's reign, there was a small side arch for pedestrians but the present single wide arch was created then. (*D.F. Vodden*)

In 1968 the Eastgate did not show very much change. (*D.F. Vodden*)

The Eastgate in 2003 is seen restored, at an estimated cost of £10 million, following the disastrous fire of September 1990. (*D.F. Vodder*

The Eastgate fire of 4 September 1990, showing the fire crews in Fore Street. Other appliances operated from the other side in High Street. The fire may have been caused by faulty electrical wiring in an office. (*Barry Weekes/Totnes Image Bank*)

distant view of the Eastgate fire was taken from the Cherry Cross area. (*A.T. Lincoln*)

picture appeared on the front page
Herald Express on 4 September
under the headline: 'TOTNES
NO HEARTBREAK – Gutted! The
of Totnes was ripped out early
. . .' This view from the High
side illustrates the intensity of the
which was attended by well over
remen. Devon's fire chief, Neil
gton, personally led the massive
tion – the biggest in the county
Dingle's Plymouth store was
yed. The cost of restoration was
ually to be about £10 million.
ditor, *Herald Express*)

The south side of Fore Street from t[ ]
Eastgate, 1983. (*A.T. Lincoln*)

The south side of Fore Street through the
Eastgate, 2000. Scaffolding can be seen on the
front of the Elizabethan House Museum as can
a considerable extension of the double yellow
lines. (*D.F. Vodden*)

75 Fore Street was already experiencing traffic problems, and little has changed in that respect.
odden)

Left: The Brutus Stone pictured in 1985 marks the place where legend says Brutus of Troy set foot on dry land, *c.* 1170 BC, uttering the words, 'Here I stand and here I rest, And this place shall be called Totnes'! A more prosaic explanation is that, when it stood 18 inches higher, officials stood on it to utter announcements. This was known as 'bruiting' in Tudor times. (*D.F. Vodden*)

Right: No. 70 Fore Street is one of the finest restored Elizabethan town houses in the country. It was built in about 1575 for Walter Kelland, a wealthy merchant. Coming on the market in 1958, it was restored and opened as a museum in 1961. In 1991 the Elizabethan museum mounted an exhibition to commemorate the birth of Charles Babbage, inventor of the first automatic calculator, who was born on Boxing Day 1791. (*D.F. Vodden*)

e are some traces of German bombing raids. The lower end of Priory Avenue was untouched and sists completely of pre-war houses. (*D.F. Vodden*)

g one daylight raid in 1942 the upper end of Priory Avenue was hit, and this picture shows the new s which were built as replacements. (*D.F. Vodden*)

While I was at King Edward's School, soon after the war, there were many traces of wartime activity in
South Hams. Salcombe and East Portlemouth had small slipways which we were told had been use
launch craft for D-Day in 1944. A large area was evacuated in November 1943 to be a training area fc
forces. Slapton was used for rehearsals for the future landings on the Normandy beaches. This Sher
tank had capsized off the beach and, having been recovered, serves as a memorial to 700 US men who
during a night exercise. (*D.F. Vodden*)

Opposite: Set up by the US government, Slapton Memorial is a 'thank you' to the thousands of villager.
were evacuated from their homes in 1943 to provide the training area. *Inset:* Detail on the Sl.
memorial. (*Both D.F. Vodden*)

The village of Blackawton was on the northern edge of the training area of 1943–4. The Normandy Arms was re-named in memory of those days. (*D.F. Vodden*)

In Blackawton the pre-war design of school sign has been retained. (*D.F. Vodden*)

ght: Before the evacuation Exeter Cathedral
chitect Herbert Read supervised the
smantling of the carved screen in
ackawton Church. After the war the choir
screen beetle damage was repaired at the
expense of the Pilgrim Trust. (*D.F. Vodden*)

low: Recently this memorial to the
evacuation of 1943–4 has been installed on a
windowsill in the church. Cyril Northcott,
who is now ninety-four years old, served on
both the Transport Committee and the Devon
War Agriculture Committee. He also supplied
trucks to help move some of the 3,000
animals who were evacuated with their
belongings at six weeks' notice. (*D.F. Vodden*)

THIS STONE COMMEMORATES
THE 50th ANNIVERSARY
OF THE TOTAL EVACUATION OF
BLACKAWTON PARISH IN 1943/4
TO ENABLE THE U.S. FORCES
TO TRAIN FOR THE
D-DAY LANDINGS IN FRANCE
AND OUR GRATITUDE
FOR SACRIFICES MADE.
ERECTED IN 1994 BY SOME OF THOSE
EVACUATED AND OTHER
PARISHIONERS AND FRIENDS.

The former village school at Cornworthy is now the Village Hall. My late grammar schoolfriend Bryan White remembered it was machine-gunned during a German daylight raid while the staff were having a tea break and the children were locked out at playtime. Apart from some grazed knees, fortunately no-one was injured. (*D.F. Vodden*)

It is still possible to see bullet scars on the wall of the building. (*D.F. Vodden*)

3

King Edward VI Grammar School

The former King Edward VI Grammar School's School House, now known as The Mansion, covered with ivy in the 1970s. Built in 1795, it became the school in 1897. (*D.F. Vodden*)

This portrait of King Edward VI, painted on copper, was presented to C.F. Rea, headmaster, on 23 October 1899 by Dr W.B. Kellock and used to be displayed in the headmaster's study. (*D.F. Vodden*)

The front door of School House, 1968. In 1... the Grammar School, Girls' High School Redworth Secondary Modern School w... combined to form King Edward VI Com... hensive School. In 1972 the school move... new buildings on the Ashburton Road. Mansion is now a base for Commu... Education. (*D.F. Vodden*)

The school badge is based on that of the town with the addition of the motto 'Scientiae Turrim Fortissimam Claves Aperiunt', which translates as 'The keys of knowledge open the strongest gate'. (*D.F. Vodden*)

I took this view of the rear of School House on 16 May 1947, when it was not only protected by slate shingling, but also had a protected way into the rear door past the headmaster's study window. (*D.F. Vodden*)

The fives courts in 1947. The smaller one, on the right, often served as the nets for playground cricket in the evenings. Behind the high wall on the left used to stand the *Totnes Times* printing works. (*D.F. Vodden*)

The fives courts in 2003 are due for demolition. It is hoped that a town library building will replace them and the former sixth form building behind them. The small court had been converted to a climbing wall in recent years but has now been declared unsafe by the Health and Safety Executive. (*D.F. Vodden*)

The *Totnes Times* left its premises in 1980. Its former site, over the wall on the left of King Edward VI's playground, has been redeveloped for housing and is now known as Times Mews. The former front office is now an estate agent. (*D.F. Vodden*)

rtrait of C.D.T. Owen, my headmaster. Having
eviously been sixth form master and taught maths
Blundell's, Tiverton, he served as headmaster at
tnes from 1935 to 1960. He died prematurely of
ncer at fifty-seven and is commemorated by a
que in St Mary's parish church. (*D.F. Vodden*)

H.R. Howard was Latin and Divinity master and
housemaster at the original Kennicott, 47 Fore
Street. A long-serving member of staff from 1919
to 1954, he maintained a close interest in the Old
Totnesian Society and took part regularly in the
London reunions until his death in his nineties.
This portrait by local artist Victor Elford was
presented to him by the Society to mark his
eightieth birthday in 1970. (*D.F. Vodden*)

Lucas Foster at his desk in 1950. He was a brilliant math master. It was he who told the form to dive under their desks when some German planes bombed Priory Avenue in October 1942. All that the boys could see of him at th time was the top of his bald head from under his desk! (*D.F. Vodden*)

The School Hall. This was not only used for Assembly, but also as a form room, hence the desks in foreground of the picture. This was taken by Anthony B. Treacher in 1953 with a hand-held box car Behind the dais is the school badge and over the door a caribou head with horns. This head was pres in 1897 by old boy Sir William Whiteway (1828–1908), a farmer's son from Littlehempston who Premier of Newfoundland for three terms. (*A.B. Treacher*)

Chemistry Laboratory used to be under the School Hall, 1930s. (*OTS Collection*)

The Physics Laboratory was on the ground floor to the right of the main staircase leading up to the School Hall, 1930s. (*OTS Collection*)

Charles Babbage was an old boy of the scho
where he spent his formative years before goi
on to Trinity College Cambridge. He is known
the father of the modern computer through h
'Difference Engine'. His name was given
one of the four houses at the scho
(KEVIC

Charles Babbage's bust at King Edward VI
Community College, Ashburton Road, was unveiled
on the 200th anniversary of his birth – Boxing Day
1991 – by Old Boy and former mayor, W.C. Bennett
MBE. (*D.F. Vodden*)

814 Babbage married Georgina Whitmore of Dudmaston, near Bridgnorth, Shropshire. The house now
ngs to the National Trust. (*D.F. Vodden*)

Cricket 1st XI in 1943 when Derek Major was Captain. He was Captain of Soccer at the same time.
ntly he is Honorary Secretary of the Old Totnesians and can claim to have been a member for over
years as can be seen from his OTS tie in the picture! (*D.D. Major*)

Upper Va in 1943 with their form master C.H. Phelps, who taught English. He joined the staff in 1914 returned after war service to complete a total of forty-one years. (*D.D. Major*).

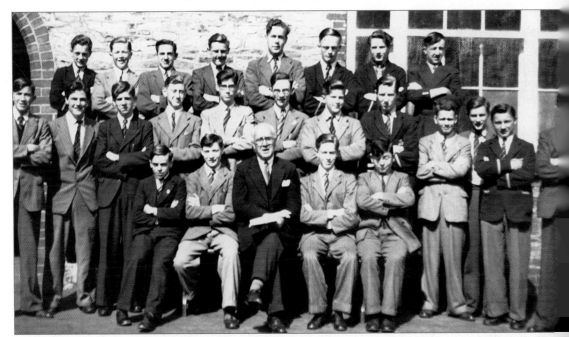

I took this picture of Upper Va in 1950 on delayed action which meant I had to move smartly from camera to the far right of the picture. C.H. Phelps had continued to be form master. Back row, left to Joint, Dommett, Endacott, Anderson, White, Sherwill, Bonner, Mayne. Middle row: Frampton, Miners, -?-, Thomas, Crook, Labdon, Irish, Keate, Jonas, Diffey, Vodden. Front row: Gosling, Evans, Mr C.H. P James, -?-. (*D.F. Vodden*)

...otographed this group of Kennicott boarders with Mr H.R. Howard in the walled garden behind the fives ...ts. (*D.F. Vodden*)

...formers sitting on the flat roof of the boiler house behind the fives courts and below the School Hall ...cape, 1951. Back row, left to right: Bickford, White, Labdon. Front row: Allnatt, Vodden, J.C. Vickery, ... (*D.F. Vodden*)

The Old Totnesian Society reunion, 1946. The masters include H.R. Howard, E.S. Smee, C.H. Phelps and B.M.E. Guy, and, of course, C.D.T. Owen. (*D.D. Major*)

This was a group of Boy Scouts in a Gang Show, 1947. Although they were mainly 1st Totnes (King Edward VI School) Troop they were supplemented by some 3rd Totnes Sea Scouts, including Donald Moffat in the centre. Born on Boxing Day 1930, from school he went to RADA. His first stage part was first messenger in *Macbeth* in 1954, and he has since gone on to become a successful Hollywood film actor, played President Bennett in *Clear and Present Danger* (1994) and also acted in episodes of *Star Trek*. (*Nicholas Horne/Totnes Image Bank*)

...uts on a tractor in 1948 at one of our ...quent weekend camps at Salcombe. Left to ...ht: J. Walden, G. Pickard, M. Anderson, ...ilcox. T. East is in front. (*D.F. Vodden*)

...uts at a weekend camp at Dartington, 1949. ... walked there with our trek cart which later ...ed as a dining table. P.H. (Pop) Rowland, ...tmaster, is on the right. (*D.F. Vodden*)

Fortnightly summer camps took place in the school holidays and here is a group halfway up Snowdon in 1949 or 1950. (*D.F. Vodden*)

While we were camping at Gilwell in Essex we visited the Festival of Britain where I took this picture in 1951. (*D.F. Vodden*)

Beginners were taught swimming in the leat which still runs from the head of the weir to the former Harris's Bacon Factory. This picture dates from the 1930s. (*D.D. Major*)

Able swimmers were allowed to swim in the Dart above the weir. Diving was from the branch of a large tree. (*D.F. Vodden*)

A couple of local girls can just be seen swimming above the weir, continuing the custom even in 2003. (*D.F. Vodden*)

Colts Rugby XV of 1949 with Mr Farrow, Art Master, outside the School Pavilion. (*Nicholas Horne/ Image Bank*)

by 1st XV of 1950 with P.H. Rowland (English) on the right and P.O. Hawke (History) on the left. Back row, to right: C.R. Drew, D.F. Vodden, M.D. Soper. Third row: R.M. Schofield, M.F. Green, J.L. Wooster, M.J. ~will, P.D. Wood. Second row: H.M. Evans, M.J. Bennett, P.E. Morrison (captain), M.D. Anderson (secretary), Bennett. Front row: D. Harris, J. Silcox, W.J. Miners, P.J. Pinney. (*Nicholas Horne/Totnes Image Bank*)

The Second School adjacent to the Guildhall from which the school moved to the Mansion in 1887. These old buildings were acquired by the County Council for £167 to be transformed into a police station. (*KEVICC*)

The present college, at Ashburton Road since 1972, as seen from the Sports Field. This is a rear view of Ariel Centre and main reception; a block designed by Harrison Sutton Partnership. (*Celia Clarke*)

In connection with the twinning of Totnes with Vire in Normandy, exchanges take place between stu... from the towns. This is a group of KEVICC Year 9 students in front of Caen Town Hall, 2003. (*KEVICC*)

Floreat Totnesia!

In Totnes Town in days of old
There lived a Norman Baron bold,
A doughty knight, yet good withal,
Who built our Priory's hallow'd hall;
And here it was by monks' good deed,
That Totnes boys learnt how to read.

When Bluff King Hal had reigned awhile.
The monks were forced to quit our isle;
His son, King Edward, on the throne,
The Priory Hall became our own:
Here 'neath the Mayor and Council's sway
Our School was kept for many a day.

Then let us sing a verse today,
In praise of those who've passed away,
The mayors, the masters, and the boys,
Who've known our sorrows and our joys,
Let's think of each whose worthy name
Is graven on the roll of fame.

As man was questing into space
A merger of three schools took place;
Thus Totnes High and Redworth too
Help raise King Edward's banner blue;
Now boys and girls from far and wide
Pursue their learning side by side.

And whereso'er this song is sung,
By past or present, old or young,
In Totnes town or far away,
Where snow or sunshine holds its way,
Be this our boast where'er we meet,
We'll greet as brothers brothers greet.

Vivat, floreat Totnesia!
Crescat, floreat Totnesia!
In saecula-permulta,
Floreat Totnesia!

nt: The school song was written by C.F. Rea
...dmaster 1896–1915) and set to a tune he heard
...le on holiday in the Tyrol. It outlines the history of
...school, and the amalgamation of the three schools
...rm the present college is described in the
...ltimate verse. (*KEVICC*)

w: The late Stanley Caldwell, Sixth Form Master
...French Master, drawn by Colin Bigwood, Head of
... Mr Caldwell was one of the grammar school
...ers who continued on the staff when the schools
...lgamated. (*Chris Bigwood*)

The Staff of KEVICC in casual dress on Sports Day, 2003. During my time, there were only 17 member staff teaching about 300 boys. (Courtesy Totnes Tim

Luke Chadwick, aged twelve, continues the stron tradition of mathematics achievement. After competing against 210,000 school children in th Junior Maths Challenge he was chosen to attend Junior Mathematical Olympiad organised by the Mathematics Trust in 2003. (Courtesy Totnes Tim

Similarly, Year 12 student, Peter Stilwell, another high achiever, was one of just four to be chosen from a national field to represent the UK at the Harry Messell International Science School at the University of Sydney in July 2003. *(VICC)*

Dinner and Reunion to celebrate the 450th year of the granting of King Edward VI's Charter, 28 June. Left to right: Mrs Moylan-Jones, Mayor's Consort Bill Bennett MBE, Mayor Cllr Judy Westacott, President OTS Peter Moore, Mrs Moore. *(D.F. Vodden)*

Stephen Jones, Principal KEVICC, Mrs Jones, Rear Admiral Roger Moylan-Jones, Mrs Moylan-Jones, Bennett and the Mayor. (*D.F. Vodden*)

Mrs Moore, Hon. Secretary OTS Derek D. Major, Mrs Major, Toastmaster Robert Hooper, Mrs H (*D.F. Vodden*)

4

High Street & Above

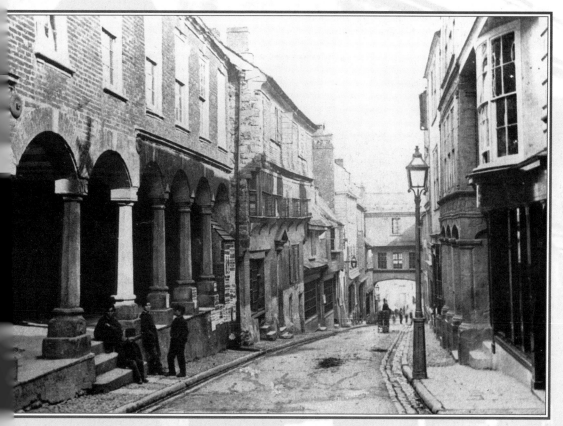

The Church Walk, with its pillars, stood above Eastgate until it was dismantled in 1878.
It had been given to the town by former Mayor Richard Lee in 1616. Some of the pillars,
including two inscribed with his name, now stand outside the Guildhall.
(A.T. Lincoln collection)

Eastgate post-1878, when the town had erected a clock and bell turret vane. (*A.T. Lincoln collection*)

The Dart Vale Hunt setting off through the Eastgate on Boxing Day 1983. (A.T. Lincoln)

e faithfully restored former Millbay ndry became the office of the Bradford Bingley Building Society. It is seen here in 1980s. (*A.T. Lincoln*)

re parked outside the church and alongside the Bradford & Bingley Building Society in the High Street y-three years later. (*D.F. Vodden*)

Looking up the High Street at the Butterwalk, 1985. Most slate shingling is plain and rectangular, but there are some rows of scalloped-edged slates. (*D.F. Vodden*)

A few miles downriver, Dartmouth also has a Butterwalk, seen here in 1968. More timbers are expos the first floor than at Totnes. (*D.F. Vodden*)

Civic Hall and Square in 1985 on a non-market day. It was designed by Professor Jellicoe, the Guildford ᵃitect, and opened in 1962. The whole area used to be occupied by a larger combined Civic Hall and ᵏet Hall until a fire destroyed it in 1955. (*D.F. Vodden*)

ᵀotnes Town Arms on the wall ᵉ Civic Hall, 2000. The town ᵈ to be a borough as the ᵗ of local government changes 74. With Barnstaple, it was ᶠ the oldest boroughs in ᵻ, dating from the late ninth ᵗʳy. (*D.F. Vodden*)

Following a visit to Volendam in Holland by Claude Taylor, chief *Totnes Times* reporter, the Elizabet
Market was devised and opened in May 1970. It still thrives, as can be seen in this 1985 view. Roy I
is the monk, and Frances Farquhar the Tudor lady. (*A.T. Lincoln*)

A corner of the market in 1985 with Birdwood House in the background. (*A.T. Lincoln*)

Peter Randall acting as Elizabethan Society Crier at a Tuesday Market in 1985. (*A.T. Lincoln*)

In the shadow of the Civic Hall is the Saturday Market in the 1980s. (*A.T. Lincoln*)

A Saturday Market
reflected in a convex
mirror (*A.T. Lincoln*)

A pianist entertaining in a Saturday market. (*A.T. Lincoln*)

Saturday Market with the ramp up to the Civic Hall in the background, 2003. (*D.F. Vodden*)

The Mayor, Bill Bennett MBE, reviving the custom of throwing pennies to children in the crowd, 19
(*W.C. Bennett*)

Swallowfields residents celebrate Queen Elizabeth II's Silver Jubilee with a street party, 1977. (*W.C. Benr*

The Residents of Swallowfields

Present this Certificate

TO

Cllr. Bill Bennett - Mayor of Totnes

TO COMMEMORATE

The Swallowfields Celebrations

OF

Queen Elizabeth II Silver Jubilee

1952 - 1977

The Swallowfields certificate presented to the mayor in 1977. (*W.C. Bennett*)

Grove School's Silver Jubilee celebrations in the castle grounds, 1977. (*W.C. Bennett*)

The High Street with Haymans at no. 42 alongside the Market and Civic Hall, 1950. The hall was bu
down in 1955. (*D.F. Vodden*)

In 2000 the Totnes Bookshop occupies the site of the former Haymans shop. (*D.F. Vodden*)

ɔk this view of the Butterwalk in 1950 from a viewpoint alongside the Midland Bank. At that time traffic ɑe High Street was two-way. (*D.F. Vodden*)

ʒutterwalk from a similar viewpoint, 2000. The bank is shrouded in scaffolding. (*D.F. Vodden*)

The Butterwalk from across the High Street, 1968. (*D.F. Vodden*)

The Midland Bank and Butterwalk, 1982. The HSBC logo had not yet arrived. (*D.F. Vodden*)

Butterwalk, *c.* 1900. This view reveals that the building on the left was a shop long before it
ame the Midland Bank. (*A.T. Lincoln collection*)

enamed bank, HSBC, and the Butterwalk, 2000. (*D.F. Vodden*)

Looking up the High Street towards the Narrows and the entrance to the former Tucker's Toffee factory, *c.* 1950. (*E. Morrison/Totnes Image Bank*)

The former Tucker's Toffee factory site in 2003, showing its redevelopment as housing named Castle Court. (*D.F. Vodden*)

Above: A view of the Narrows looking towards the castle, 1976. *(D.F. Vodden)*

The Narrows looking towards the castle, 1980s. *(A.T. Lincoln)*

The Narrows from the same viewpoint in 2(shows little change in the buildings but a changes in occupancy. *(D.F. Vodden)*

The Narrows looking the other way up towards the Kingsbridge Road, 1980s. *(A.T. Lincoln)*

The Rotherfold, 2000. This used to be the site of the cattle market. I can remember attending here when the mayor read the proclamation of the accession of Queen Elizabeth II in 1952. (*D.F. Vodden*)

This picture of the corner of the Rotherfold illustrates how shops change occupancy quite regularly while the streetscape stays the same. (*D.F. Vodden*)

The Totnes Carnival, 1993. The parade always starts at the top of the town and comes through the Narrows, High Street, Eastgate, Fore Street and ends on The Plains. (*A.T. Lincoln*)

Another float in the carnival procession 1993. (*A.T. Lincoln*)

ve: Mayor Mrs Margaret Stone in the procession, 1994. (*A.T. Lincoln*)

w: Midsummer Madness was the name taken for the celebrations in 1994. (*A.T. Lincoln*)

A fire-eating demonstration outside the bank in 1994. (*A.T. Lincoln*)

The Totnes Town Band in the Narrows, 1994. (*A.T. Lincoln*)

or Councillor Miss J. Westacott and her consort Bill Bennett MBE at the carnival in 2003. (*D.F. Vodden*)

otnes Town Band striding down High Street at the 2003 carnival. (*D.F. Vodden*)

Totnes Fire Brigade collecting for charity at the carnival, 2003. (*D.F. Vodden*)

The Ashburton Cricket Club float with Queen at the carnival, 2003. (*D.F. Vodden*)

5

Church, Guildhall & Castle

Totnes dominated by its castle and St Mary's Priory Church in 1981. (*A.T. Lincoln*)

This is the east end of St Mary's Church in 1950. Since then the churchyard has had the headstones removed. (*D.F. Vodden*)

ght: The east end of the
urch in 1982 reveals
e lawn effect of the
urchyard and the new
enue of young trees.
F. Vodden)

low: The east end of
Mary's Church in
00, fifty years after my
liest picture.
F. Vodden)

The main entrance to St Mary's Church, 1982. It was built between 1420 and 1455 and the whole church dates from the same century apart from the north aisle, added in 1824. (*D.F. Vodden*)

A view of St Mary's nave and screen, 1950. Grammar school boarders used to sit in the pews on the right at the rear of the church. The two large velvet cushions were on the lecterns of the Corporation pews and used to support the mayor's and mayoress's large Books of Common Prayer. St Leonard's chapel on the left contained the organ at that time. (*D.F. Vodden*)

Mary's church nave in a picture postcard shows the extent of the fine fifteenth-century stone screen. *holas Horne/Totnes Image Bank)*

organ was moved to the rear of the church in 1959, back to where it had originally been housed en 1861 and 1889. The nave and screen remain unaltered in this 2003 view. (*D.F. Vodden*)

Some detail of the very fine stone screen Totnes, built in 1459. (*D.F. Vodden*)

Particularly at Foundation Services, Grammar School boys sat in the choir stalls. The last summer I was there, we sang Roger Quilter's *Non Nobis Domine* and I remember sitting looking at this rood loft staircase which had been constructed during Sir Gilbert Scott's 1867 restoration. (*D.F. Vodden*)

George's chapel is at the right-
nd end of the screen. This
otograph dates from 1950.
llop shells carved around the
rway suggest this also had some
nection with St James.
E. Vodden)

St George's chapel, 2000. The chandelier no
longer has real candles in it and the prie-dieus
have been replaced with a simple altar rail.
The Mothers' Union banner has wording from
St Mary's ancient seal embroidered on it.
(D.F. Vodden)

Against the south wall stands Walter Smythe's tomb. A merchant in tin and cloth, he was the second richest trader after John Giles in the 1520s. After the 1536 dissolution the priory he played a leading part in acquiring much of its property. He gave the priory site to the Crown who incorporated it within the borough in 1553. The Guildhall and Grammar School were subsequently built there. (*D.F. Vodden*)

The mayor, Bill Bennett MBE, and council emerging from St Mary's after the Civic Service, 1977. (*W.C. B*

I took this picture of the Guildhall in 1950. I think it is my school friend Keate who is standing by one of the pillars. (*D.F. Vodden*)

Not much had changed at the Guildhall when I took this in 1968. Some hanging baskets had been added to cheer it up. (*D.F. Vodden*)

The Guildhall in 2000 had a new street lamp, troughs of flowers, a seat and lots of moss on the cobbles. (*D.F. Vodden*)

The Guildhall Chamber has an inscription relating to its founding by Edward VI in 1553. This is whe mayor-making ceremony continues to be held. Senior Grammar School boys attended and the schoc granted a Mayor's Day holiday, usually added on to a half-term. (*A.T. Lincoln*)

Bennett MBE, mayor in 1977, emerging from the Guildhall after Mayor-making. (*W.C. Bennett*)

Norman Castle's shell keep dominates the town. I took this picture on the way back from the sports
one Wednesday afternoon in 1949. (*D.F. Vodden*)

Above: The castle was first built in 1070 in timber by Judael, the second largest Norman landowner in county. In the fourteenth century the Zouche family rebuilt it in stone, as we see in my picture of 19 (*D.F. Vodden*)

Below: A Tudor play in the bailey of the castle grounds in the 1980s. A pageant celebrating the impor events of 1553 also took place here in 1953. (*A.T. Lincoln*)

ve: Another scene from the play in the 1980s. (*A.T. Lincoln*)

ow: The castle's site has a good view of the town and of the River Dart. Here in July 1985 the church is ...minent. (*A.T. Lincoln*)

Above: The church and town from the castle fifteen years later shows little change from the previous p
except for the growth of trees. (*D.F. Vodden*)

Below: The River Dart can be clearly seen from the castle battlements in 1968. (*D.F. Vodden*)

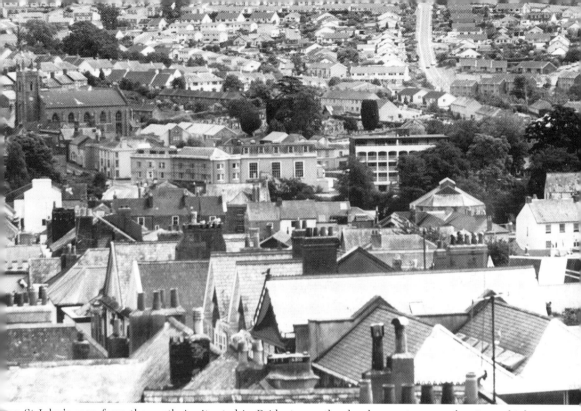

ve: St John's seen from the castle is situated in Bridgetown, the development across the river which was ...ted originally by the Dukes of Somerset. This view is from 1985. (*A.T. Lincoln*)

w: A telephoto view of the River Dart from the castle in July 1985 shows Reeves' Timber on the quay ... new housing development down the hill towards Warlands. (*A.T. Lincoln*)

Above: I photographed the River Dart from Kingsbridge Road in 1948. This particular view has altered little since it is almost out of reach of housing development. *(D.F. Vodden)*

Left: Totnes Bridge and the new Brutus Bridge under construction from Kingsbridge Hill, June 1982. *(A.T. Lincoln)*

Right: Both river bridges from Kingsbridge Hill, June 1983. *(A.T. Lincoln)*

Totnes town and the railway static
from beyond Chateau Bellevue (wh
is in the foreground, partly hidden
trees), along the Newton Abbot R
1949. White smoke or steam can
seen rising from a locomotive at t
station. St Mary's Church is in the
centre of the picture. (*D.F. Vodden*)

The station, seen from the castle
2000, no longer has steam rising
from main-line locomotives. The
creamery or milk factory chimne
still dominates the centre of the
picture. (*D.F. Vodden*)

: 2000 view of the station from the castle illustrates even better the close proximity of the milk factory to the ...on. Originally land was purchased from the railway on which to build the factory. It was known as Daw's ...mery when I was a boy but is now Unigate, and one of the biggest employers in the town. (*D.F. Vodden*)

...s station from the road bridge, 1948. It stood on the main GWR line from Paddington to Plymouth. ...he right-hand side there are a couple of steam shunting locomotives. Many day boys used to travel ...d the locomotive *Bulliver* from the Buckfastleigh direction in my time at the school. (*D.F. Vodden*)

Totnes station, July 1985. There has been considerable redevelopment of the station buildings. (*D.F. Vodd*

The station, 2000. Weeds seem to be encroaching on the left-hand side and there is no longer any s
steam. (*D.F. Vodden*)

...es station was quite transformed in this modern view with a Virgin train in 2000. (*D.F. Vodden*)

...m train on the then Dart Valley Railway line from Buckfastleigh, April 1988. (*A.T. Lincoln*)

A Dart Valley Railway locomotive at Staverton Bridge station, October 1995. (*A.T. Lincoln*)

The Buckfastleigh–Totnes line is now run as the South Devon Railway. Dart Valley Railway now refers to Paignton–Kingswear line. A tanker here in 2003 is changing from the rear to the front of a train at Totnes Littlehempston station. It was formerly known confusingly as Totnes Riverside station. (*D.F. Vodden*)

6

Dartington, Buckfastleigh
& Beyond

Dartington Hall was derelict when Leonard and Dorothy Elmhirst bought it in 1925 and established forestry and other rural crafts and industries to reverse unemployment in the area. The hall had been built in the fourteenth century by the Earl of Huntingdon and was subsequently bought by the Champernownes in 1559. *(Totnes Image Bank)*

The very attractive thatched Cott Inn near Dartington was originally built in 1320. I frequently passed it on Grammar School boarders' Sunday afternoon walks. Eventually, I fulfilled an ambition by staying there with my wife in 1982. (*D.F. Vodden*)

The Cott Inn has become ever more popular. It was difficult to photograph because of customers' cars in 2003. (*D.F. Vodden*)

rtington Banqueting Hall is pictured during a lull in activity at the annual Way with Words Conference 2003. The building was described by Nikolaus Pevsner as 'Among the finest of its date in the whole of gland'. Arthur Lincoln's daughter Celia held her reception here after her wedding at St Mary's Church, tnes, on 24 June 1993. (*D.F. Vodden*)

tington Hall is internationally famous as a centre for the arts. As senior boys we often went to the Barn atre to see performances of plays such as *The Cherry Orchard* by Anton Chekhov. I was also taken to a rse on Greek theatre by Stan Caldwell when I was in the sixth form. (*A.T. Lincoln*)

Above: This view looks from the Dartington Hall Banqueting Hall porch across the courtyard towards the buildings by the main entrance. *(A.T. Lincoln)*

Right: Set in the Banqueting Hall porch is this White Hart roof boss, pictured in 1968. It reminds us that the original builder, the Earl of Huntingdon, was half-brother to Richard II whose badge it was. *(D.F. Vodden)*

Dartington Hall doorway in 1968. *(D.F. Vodden)*

The same doorway, seen in 2003, shows only slight change. This is one of the attractions of Dartington: it is largely unchanging, yet well-maintained. *(D.F. Vodden)*

Above: The jousting ground in Dartington Hall, 1980s. (*A.T. Lincoln*)

Below: The open air theatre at Dartington, 1968. (*D.F. Vodden*)

ve: The rear of Dartington Hall from the open air theatre, 1968.

ow: The trees have grown somewhat in this picture of Dartington Hall from the same viewpoint in
3. *(Both D.F. Vodden)*

The Vodden and Galliano families descending steps in the gardens of Dartington Hall, 1968. (*D.F. Vodden*)

The swan fountain, Dartington, is positioned at the top of the flight of steps in the picture above. (*D.F. Vodden*

ot only literature conferences but also
t, especially sculpture, exhibitions take
ace in the summer at Dartington.
is piece was shown in the 1980s.
.T. Lincoln)

ong the arts, Dartington includes an
ual music festival, here housed in the
queting Hall in 1979. (A.T. Lincoln)

Here are two performers in the open air at the Dartington Music Festival, 1993. (*A.T. Lincoln*)

It is not clear whether these chefs are providing refreshments or participating in a Dartington Hall co
competition. (*A.T. Lincoln*)

Dartington Hall's 2003 Way with Words
nference, the notice on these outside stairs
ught my eye. (*D.F. Vodden*)

ies, which is only 2 miles away, can be seen
n some parts of the grounds. This photograph
taken in June 1982. (*A.T. Lincoln*)

The Totnes Show is held annually at Berry Pomeroy in fields belonging to the Duke of Somerset. Th
ponies were ready for judging at a show in the 1980s. (*A.T. Lincoln*)

Equestrian activities at the Totnes Show include jumping. (*A.T. Lincoln*)

e is a very smart pony and trap at the Totnes
w about twenty-five years ago. (*A.T. Lincoln*)

ng been painstakingly restored since 1884,
fast Abbey, originally founded in 1018 in the
of Cnut, is now a successfully run religious
nunity. This is the west front of the church in
. (*P.E. Vodden*)

Buckfast Abbey west front ten years later shows that no more than flowerbed designs seem to have changed. This is the only English medieval abbey to have been restored to its original purpose. (*D.F. Vodden*)

Buckfast Abbey west front has low-maintenance lawns in front of it in 2003. There are, however, rose gardens, herb gardens and a very modern conference centre alongside, but just out of the picture. (*D.F. Vodden*)

KEEP LEFT

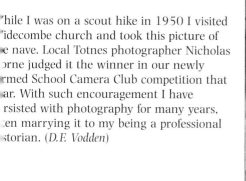

hile I was on a scout hike in 1950 I visited
idecombe church and took this picture of
e nave. Local Totnes photographer Nicholas
orne judged it the winner in our newly
rmed School Camera Club competition that
ar. With such encouragement I have
rsisted with photography for many years,
en marrying it to my being a professional
storian. (*D.F. Vodden*)

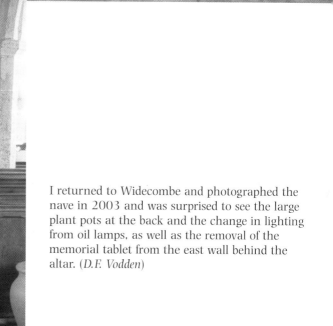

I returned to Widecombe and photographed the
nave in 2003 and was surprised to see the large
plant pots at the back and the change in lighting
from oil lamps, as well as the removal of the
memorial tablet from the east wall behind the
altar. (*D.F. Vodden*)

ACKNOWLEDGEMENTS

While many of the photographs are my own, I am grateful to the following people who have provided further pictures and information:

W.C. (Bill) Bennett, MBE, Honoured Citizen and three times mayor, who has shared his extensive local knowledge as well as supplying pictures from his collection and the Foreword to this book; Colin Bigwood, the former Head of Art, and Celia Clarke at KEVICC; David Harris OBE of the Old Totnesian Society; Mr and Mrs Tony Highfield; Stephen Jones, the Principal of KEVICC; Alan Langmaid, the Administrator of the Elizabethan Museum; Mrs Vi Lincoln for giving me full access to her collection of her late husband Arthur's excellent photographs; Derek D. Major, Hon. Secretary of the Old Totnesian Society; Cyril Northcott; Doug Northcott of Northcott Photographic; Nick Pile at The Mansion; Val Price at Totnes Image Bank; Paddy Reardon, Archivist at KEVICC; Tom Maughan of Totnes Rotary Club; Jackie Smith, MD of the *Totnes Times*; the late Bob Shayler; the late Paul Twine; Mrs Mary Twine; Barrington Weekes of Totnes Image Bank and my schoolfriend, the late Bryan D. White, for information and encouragement.